Marki

Marki

LIFE IN A BRONZE AGE CYPRIOT VILLAGE

David Frankel &
Jennifer M. Webb

MOUFFLON PUBLICATIONS 2008

Moufflon Publications
42 Sofouli Street
1096 Lefkosia, Cyprus

www.moufflonpublications.com
publishing@moufflon.com.cy

Copyright © David Frankel and Jennifer M. Webb 2008

All rights reserved.
No part of this book may be reproduced or transmitted in any form by any means, electronic, mechanical, photocopying, recording, or otherwise, without the prior written permission of the publisher.

ISBN 978-9963-642-28-1

Typeset by Toby Macklin in Arno Pro
www.tobymacklin.com

Printed and bound in Cyprus by Imprinta Ltd.

Acknowledgements

The research underpinning this account is the product of fifteen years of work based on our excavations at Marki. During this time we were fortunate to receive a series of grants from the Australian Research Council, and we are also heavily indebted to generations of student excavators who contributed their time, energy and enthusiasm. As with all archaeologists in Cyprus we have been generously supported by our colleagues, both Cypriot and from overseas. Of primary importance are many past and present members of the Department of Antiquities, including six Directors, Vassos Karageorghis, Athanassios Papageorgiou, Michael Loulloupis, Demos Christou, Sophocles Hadjisavvas and Pavlos Flourentzos, as well as many others, especially Evtichia Zachariou, Giorgos Georgiou, Despo Pilides, Maria Hadjicosti, Grigoris Christou and Andreas Georgiades.

For most of the object photography we are indebted to Rudy Frank and Wei Ming, who also assisted in the final design of this book.

Figure 1. Looking northeast across the main area of excavations.

A Note on Chronology

Later prehistory in Cyprus, as in surrounding countries, retains conventional divisions into designated periods despite a long-standing and widespread recognition that they are often inappropriate and inadequate. They nevertheless have value in providing a common reference to sets of material and sequences, while their absolute ages and duration will continue to be points of debate for many years to come. A broadly accepted chronology is:

Late Chalcolithic	2800 – 2400 BCE
Early Cypriot Bronze Age	2400 – 2000 BCE
Middle Cypriot Bronze Age	2000 – 1650 BCE
Late Cypriot Bronze Age	1650 – 1150 BCE

In this book we have subdivided the continuous developmental sequence of the Early and Middle Bronze Ages into five general periods, grouping finer-scale periods where divisions constructed elsewhere on the basis of typological developments cannot be discerned at Marki or more generally applied.

We also use the broad term 'prehistoric Bronze Age' to refer generally to the Early and Middle Cypriot Bronze Age where finer-level distinctions are not necessary or not possible.

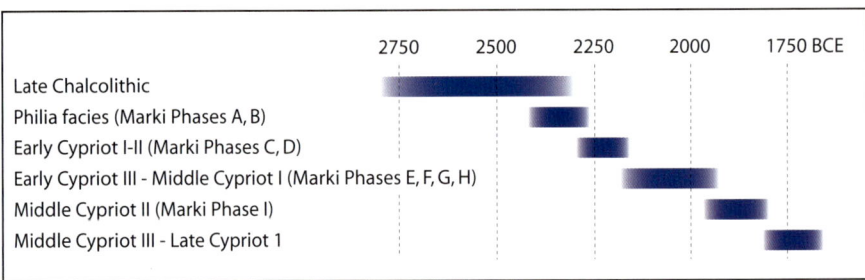

Figure 2. Chronological chart indicating the relationship between the nine Phases at Marki and main archaeological periods.

Excavations at Marki

Marki first came to the attention of archaeologists when the accidental discovery of tombs was reported to the Department of Antiquities in 1940. These tombs were part of a series of extensive cemeteries which surrounded the associated settlement at *Alonia*. All were thoroughly looted over the next 40 years, especially at times when inter-communal conflict prevented policing of the area. Many items, including well-known vessels with modelled figures, found their way into private collections, and some pieces, ostensibly from the nearby village of Kotsiatis, probably came from the Marki cemeteries.

Figure 3. Excavations in progress.

The Australian Cyprus Expedition began formal archaeological excavations at *Alonia* in 1990, with a preliminary survey of the site and the surrounding region, and continued over the next decade. In November and December each year our team of two to three dozen Australian students worked at the site and helped document the thousands of finds. Although we tested other areas our work concentrated on the north-western sector of the 5 hectare site. Here we were able to expose about 2000m^2—the largest area of a prehistoric Cypriot Bronze Age settlement to date. Of equal if not greater significance, we found evidence of continual occupation over some four or five centuries; from the foundation of the village near the very beginning of the Early Bronze Age through to its abandonment in the Middle Bronze Age. We have been able to divide this long sequence of occupation into nine Phases, each representing about two generations. It is this combination of a long history and extensive excavation that gives us the opportunity to see how an ancient village developed, to expose the nature of the life and work of its inhabitants, and to contribute to a better understanding of Cypriot prehistory more generally.

Historical Context

For the first half of the third millennium BCE all of Cyprus shared a general cultural system. Although neither static nor unchanging, these Late Chalcolithic communities maintained common elements. Settlements were relatively small, and characterised by circular houses, best exemplified at the site of Kissonerga *Mosphilia* in the south-west of the island. A wide range of crops were exploited, with agriculture based on hand tillage, presumably using hoes or similar tools. Sheep, goat and pig were herded, and wild fallow deer hunted in the forested areas. Although largely isolated from the outside world, there was some, perhaps increasing, contact with the Anatolian coast, as testified by a variety of small items, including the possible importation of copper.

The advent of the Bronze Age is identified by numerous new elements evident in the archaeological record after about 2400 BCE. These include a range of technological innovations in both domestic and other activities: so wide a range that they can only be regarded as representing the movement of people to the island from Anatolia. The stimulus for this movement is unclear, but it is likely that the search for new sources of copper was one significant factor, as for a short time Cyprus was one node in a widespread eastern Mediterranean exchange network, involving the distribution of metals and other goods.

Along with their ability to mine and process copper, these Bronze Age settlers had a fundamentally different economy from their Chalcolithic predecessors and neighbours. New breeds of sheep and, more significantly, donkeys and cattle now played a key role in agricultural practice, with the plough replacing the hoe, allowing larger areas of land to be farmed more efficiently. This led in turn to changes in settlement pattern and a marked growth in population numbers.

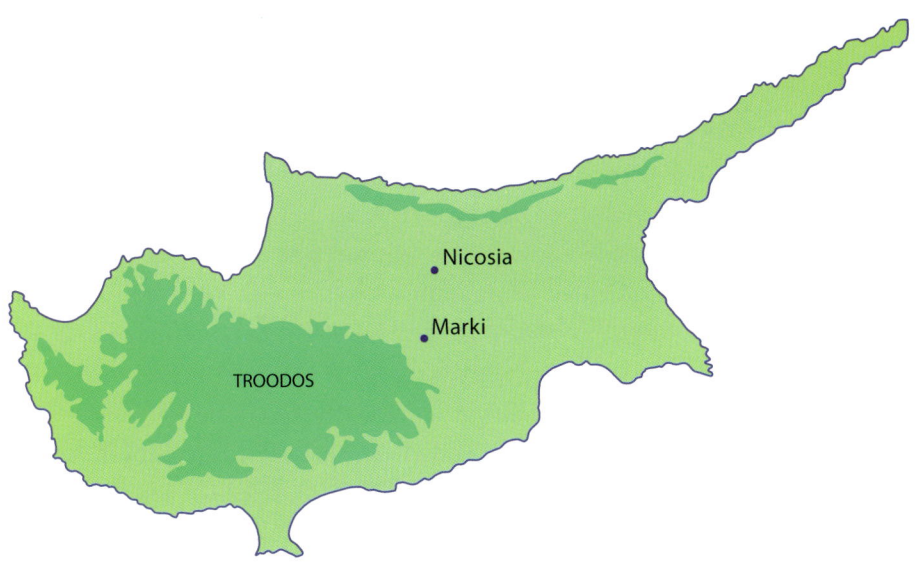

Figure 4. The location of Marki, south of Nicosia.

The process of colonisation and spread of Bronze Age people across the island is still – like so much of Cypriot prehistory – poorly understood, although, as will be seen below, Marki provides some important clues. There is no sign, however, of conflict between the indigenous Chalcolithic farmers and their new neighbours. Nevertheless, within a few generations no archaeological trace of the older way of life can be seen. Descendants of the Chalcolithic villagers had adopted all the characteristics of the Bronze Age.

The earliest Bronze Age communities (those we refer to as belonging to the Philia facies of the Early Bronze Age) shared extremely similar types and styles of artefacts, suggesting constant and close ties between different villages and regions. This unity gave way to somewhat more varied patterns in the ensuing Early Cypriot I–II period. Settlement size increased, bringing with it associated changes in the nature of relationships both within and between villages, something clearly demonstrated at Marki. These processes continued into the Early Cypriot III and subsequent Middle Cypriot I–II periods, after which time the village at Marki was abandoned. It is possible that this was related to some general and significant shifts in settlement pattern and the nature and distribution of sites. Some major centres, such as those at Nicosia and Deneia grew rapidly in size and importance, while others, like Marki, declined and were no longer occupied.

Establishing a Village

Marki was first occupied about 2300 BCE, by people we identify through their distinctive pottery and other items as belonging to the earliest period of the Bronze Age, named after the village where it was first formally described over sixty years ago as the Philia culture. Marki provides the only substantial evidence of architecture of this period, which is otherwise known only from a small number of tombs. These first inhabitants of Marki were only one or two generations removed from groups of people who had made the sea-crossing from southern Anatolia, bringing with them new technologies and ways of life. As noted above, in Cyprus they rapidly developed a widespread, uniform and distinctive material culture, binding separate villages into a close-knit network, and signalling their separation from their indigenous, Chalcolithic, neighbours.

The first people to live at Marki would have come from another village, perhaps a far larger and well established one. One possibility is a settlement currently known only from tombs, which must have existed about 15km to the north on the southern hills of Nicosia, overlooking the Pedeios River valley. It is also possible, however, that these pioneers came from the coast, where the Philia settlers first established themselves.

Why did they select Marki? The region is far from prime agricultural land, with a relatively low rainfall. This made the region unattractive for earlier, Chalcolithic occupation, but, with the newly-introduced ox and plough agriculture, more extensive areas could be brought under cultivation providing the subsistence base for a substantial and growing population. A more specific, major consideration was the proximity of copper sources, a few kilometres away. The site may therefore have been selected as being the closest area of open terrain to the more confined lands in the igneous hills. A stone mould for casting copper ingots is among the earliest artefacts found at the site, testifying to the importance of this industry from the start of the settlement.

Our first villagers – perhaps only numbering two or three dozen – would have brought with them sufficient resources to survive the first difficult pioneering years. This may not have been so unusual, as their immediate forebears had developed the strategies for successful transplantation of groups of people. They would still have needed, however, to maintain close connections with their home village – a source of supplies of food, animals and additional support – perhaps for several generations until Marki became self sufficient.

Topography and Resources

The pioneering families who first established the village selected their site near where the two major geological formations of central Cyprus meet: the ancient volcanic or igneous mineral-rich zone which makes up the Troodos Mountains and foothills, and the more geologically recent and agriculturally productive sedimentary limestones and chalks of the central plains. The area is relatively open and the village was not walled, suggesting that security was not a significant concern.

The first houses were built on the slope of a hill running down to the Alykos River. As the village expanded, occupation extended over more even ground to the south and across a gentle slope to the east through which a smaller tributary ran. The valleys and surrounding hills were originally open woodland, but over time clearance for farming and the effects of overgrazing must have gradually reduced the vegetation cover, leading to increased erosion and soil-loss. Today the area appears relatively barren and unproductive, especially during the extreme heat of mid-summer, but four thousand years ago it would have been better served by the rivers and more attractive to Bronze Age villagers.

Most of the raw materials needed for buildings, tools and utensils could be found close to the village, or within a few hours travel. Finer quality clays suitable for pottery were collected from beside the Alykos River, while coarser clays for mudbricks were readily to hand on site. Most other building material was also easily collected, with igneous boulders in the river bed and limestone slabs from the surrounding hills. In the later periods, some walls included coarse-grained calcarenite blocks brought in from ten kilometres away.

Timber for buildings may have been relatively abundant close to the site in the early days, but later, as these woodlands were cleared, larger roof beams would have had to be brought from the pine forests in the hills and even firewood may have been harder to come by. Flint for sickle-blades and light woodworking tools was readily available, although the better quality stone had to be quarried or collected at some distance from the site. Elongated basalt boulders suitable for fashioning into heavy grindstones and rubbers could be selected from those washed down the river bed; occasionally coarser-grained calcarenite was used, especially for lower grindstones, because of its abrasive qualities.

Rarer items came from further away. Dentalia and other shells used for making personal ornaments show contacts with the coast. Small pieces of picrolite came from distant sources in western Cyprus (Fig. 5). This soft blue

Figure 5. Picrolite pendants.

stone, which was used for fashioning pendants, was prized for the ease with which it could be carved and perhaps also for its symbolic significance.

It is also possible that some other commodities were regularly traded in to the village. These perhaps included salt from coastal salt pans, such as the famous ones at Larnaca, and flax from wetter areas in the larger river valleys or on the coast. Small vessels of wares not made locally suggest that other – perhaps luxury – items, such as perfumes, ointments and drugs, were also brought from other areas.

Copper, both for local use and to distribute to other areas of the island, was mined a few kilometres into the hills. It is likely that primary processing took place close to the mines, where wood for the furnaces would have been readily available. The smelted copper may then have been carried to the village to be cast into tools and ornaments or into ingots to be traded to other parts of the island.

Housing

A key to understanding the history and nature of life at Marki lies in the changing form of the built environment. Early and Middle Bronze Age houses were in some respects similar to traditional Cypriot village houses of the nineteenth and twentieth centuries. The lower courses of walls were made up of several courses of stone, with the upper sections built of mould-made mudbricks.

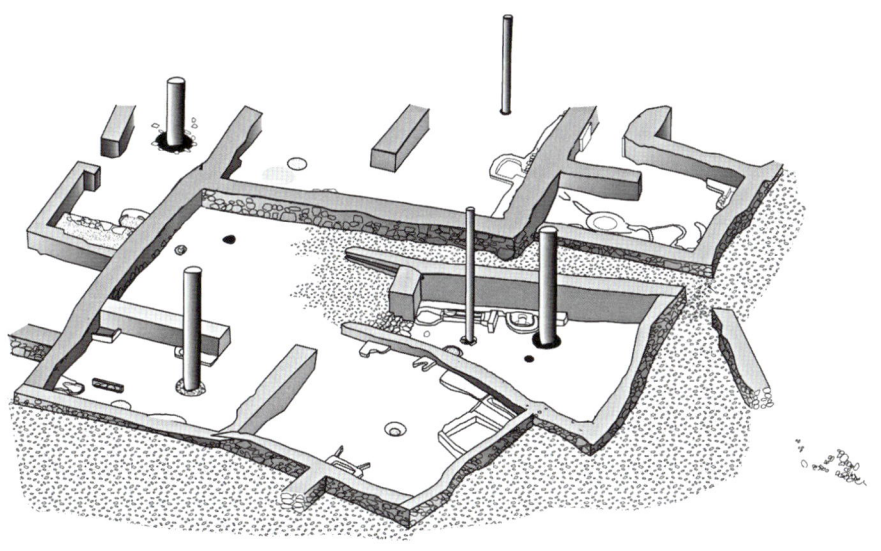

Figure 6. Schematic view of Compound 6, Phases E, F.

Figure 7. Compound 29, Phase G.

Walls were sometimes covered with a thin clay render or with white lime-wash (we have in one place the suggestion of red colouring on the wall). The roofs were probably flat, with wooden beams supporting layers of matting and packed earth. Where the span of the room required, wooden posts supported the main roof-beams. Floors were not formally constructed, but consisted of mud or clay packed hard through use and trampling, and often very unevenly worn down. Doors, probably made of wood and swung on stone pivots, closed off entry to courtyards and inner rooms.

Within the houses there was a variety of built-in fittings and features. Low, narrow plaster-covered benches lined some interior walls, perhaps serving as shelves for household items. Some benches were associated with hearths. These had small fire-boxes set into the back bench, with low semicircular or rectangular fenders (Fig. 8). Low rectangular closed clay ovens of various sizes were also built adjacent to walls (Fig. 9). Other substantial circular hollow installations made from a concretion of clay, plaster and small pebbles were set into the floor, generally alongside the walls. These may have been settings for large storage jars, or used for some other domestic purpose.

Figure 8. Plaster bench, hearth and hearth surround.   Figure 9. Clay oven.

The structure of houses varied through time and in accordance with individual circumstances, but some common themes can be identified in the 33 excavated architectural households or house compounds. Most of these compounds are comprised of two or more covered rooms set within a partly or fully enclosed courtyard and can be regarded as the domain of separate social households, or families. Our ability to trace fine-scale changes in both the structure and location of compounds through time provides an important basis for understanding the way in which people made use of space and negotiated their relationships. At Marki we have a rare opportunity to explore the social history of a village.

Architectural History

Figures 10, 11 and 12 show the changing nature of households in the excavated area of the village.

The earliest evidence we have at Marki dates from a time shortly after its foundation about 2300 BCE. The two excavated complexes of Phase A are very poorly preserved but appear to have been on the edge of the small village. To the east arrays of post holes suggest the presence of animal pens and work stations beyond the built-up area. A generation or two later, in Phase B, several new compounds were constructed. The best preserved were two-room units set within a common courtyard, used for flint-knapping, antler- and shell-working, pottery production and baking in a large oven. Sets of post holes suggest animal pens and sheds; a fence and a pithos burial mark the southern boundary, while a freestanding room in the southeast served as a storage and processing facility. These compounds appear to represent two households with separate inner rooms and shared courtyard space, forming a cooperative residential and economic unit.

As the population of the village increased, the built-up area expanded. In Phase C (Early Cypriot I), the earlier Phase B compounds were replaced by new Compounds 6 and 7. These retained the general form of covered rooms within a courtyard, which was now enclosed by a stone wall on three sides. While there was no access between these two compounds, the courtyard of one of them (Compound 6) opened onto that of the smaller Compound 8. This suggests a connection between these two households, perhaps involving the establishment by Compound 6 of an off-shoot to house an extended family unit. Other households built in Phase C are similar in structure with covered rooms set within partly walled courtyards. Although some share walls, they were clearly independent units of relatively similar size, each with a total area of about 100m².

The inhabited area expanded further in Phase D (Early Cypriot II). The greater density of housing required the establishment of a north/south laneway to provide access through this part of the settlement. While Compound 7 remained unchanged, Compound 6 was substantially modified and both Compounds 6 and 8 were now entered via a short passage from the lane. Compound 9 was restructured to become a three-roomed house entered from the laneway and a number of new compounds were built on either side of the lane. These include two-room Compounds 14 and 15 without courtyards on the west and a larger Compound 13, with two inner rooms and a courtyard, on the east. Three new compounds of the usual type were constructed in previously open space to the northeast.

In Phase E (Early Cypriot III) Compound 7 was completely walled off and reoriented to the north. In Compound 8 the two inner rooms were enlarged and a third room added to the west. Major and minor changes are also visible in the compounds to the east, where new laneways were established to provide access to compounds built at this time. This reduced reliance on the main north/south access route and arranged old compounds into new configurations.

This pattern of increasing density of occupation continued during Phase F. To the north new compounds were constructed on open ground and areas of open space between compounds were enclosed. Major changes also occurred in the centre of the area with the construction of Compound 28. This involved the partial demolition of what had previously been the interior rooms of Compound 13, creating the first standing ruins in the excavated area. At the same time a new phenomenon, that of the single-room compound appears (Compounds 23 and 24).

During Phases G (Middle Cypriot I), and increasingly thereafter, the centre of the settlement gradually shifted away from the original area, expanding toward the south-east. Our excavations show this process of local decline as compounds fell out of use and were not replaced. Compounds 6 and 7 continued to be occupied within their original boundaries and some new compounds were built (notably Compound 29), but others were reduced in size or abandoned. By Phase H the density of occupation was significantly lower in this part of the site and by Phase I (Middle Cypriot II) only three compounds were still in use. The oldest part of the village was all but abandoned.

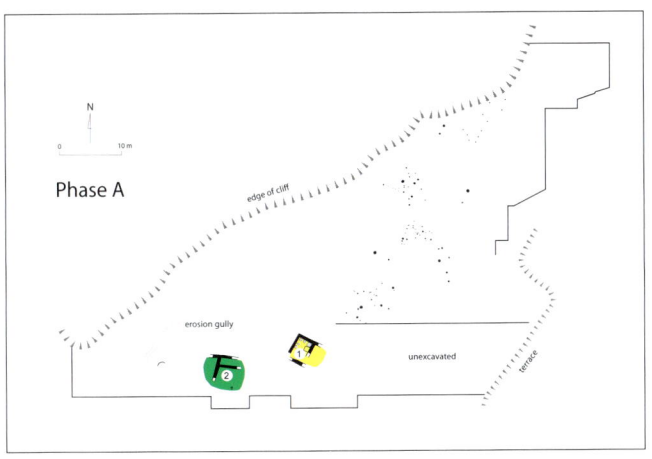
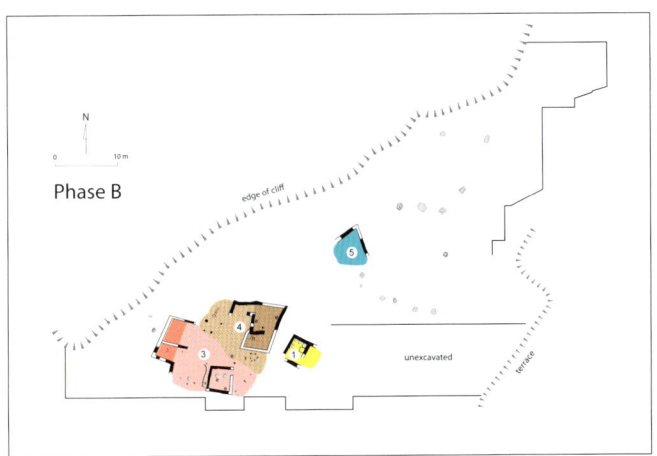
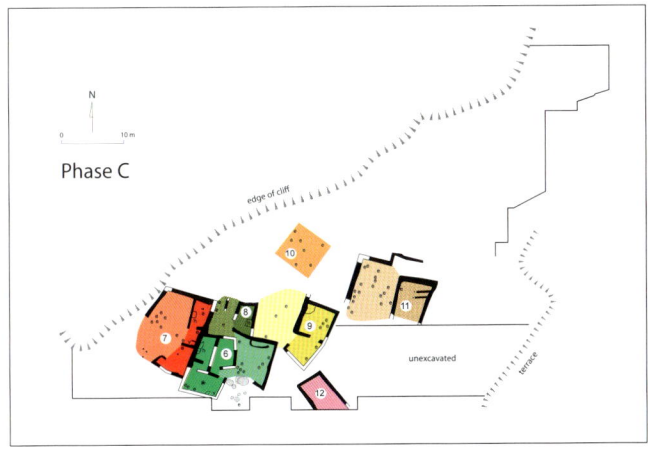

Figure 10. Households during Phases A–C.

Figure 11. Households during Phases D – F.

Figure 12. Households during Phases G – I.

The Evolving Household

Discrete house compounds with two, three or more rooms at the rear of a courtyard were clearly the standard house form at Marki from first settlement to final abandonment. Although new household types, specifically single room units and compounds with no courtyards, developed through time, the majority of compounds, particularly where these were not constrained by existing structures, took the traditional form. Also evident is an intra-site evolution from relatively open, cooperative relationships in the earliest years of occupation to an increasingly segregated, enclosed system in later periods. In Phases A and B courtyards were open or surrounded by light fences. In Phase C walls were built to close courtyards on three sides, leaving wide entrances from surrounding open space. By Phase E courtyards were fully walled with access via narrow doorways or internal passages.

Alongside these developments, interior space was progressively subdivided and access routes were increasingly formalised. The location of some facilities also changed. Animal pens and work stations, initially found in courtyards, are not present from Phase D onward. Ovens were relocated to interior rooms in Phase C and internal screen walls appear, apparently to conceal hearths from exterior view (these features are best seen in the well-preserved Compound 29). These changes may be seen as reflecting an increasing desire for household privacy and security, which is likely to have been linked with notions of private property, intergenerational inheritance and the control and manipulation of space and other resources.

These developments can be related to various installations and artefacts found in the site. In Phases A and B they suggest co-operative storage, preparation and consumption of food between several, probably kin-related households. From Early Cypriot I onward, however, staples were stored in closed courtyards and interior rooms and ovens were reduced in size and moved into kitchen extensions. At the same time decorated table ware, which had been prominent during the earliest, Philia periods of occupation, virtually disappears. This suggests that social interaction or commensality between households was more restricted in Early Cypriot I and II, in keeping with the increased architectural isolation of house compounds and the location of hearths and ovens in interior rooms.

Population and Social Relationships

How many people lived at Marki? This is not an easy question to answer for any prehistoric society, but we can be sure that the size of the village changed constantly through time. Our best estimates are based on an assessment of how many people the village lands could support, the expanding size of the settlement and the probable number of people buried in the surrounding cemeteries. These suggest that over four centuries the small founding population of no more than two or three dozen people would have grown to a sizeable community of about 400 people.

A significant factor in these estimates is the probable life expectancy and birth-rates of the time. Although direct evidence is scanty, it is most likely that few men survived beyond 40 to 45 years in age, while most women would have had little chance of reaching 35. The implications of this on the structure of individual families and social relationships within the village are profound. It is unlikely, for example, that many women would have seen their grandchildren – indeed many may not have lived to see most of their children reach adulthood. In such circumstances, it would have been common for children to be brought up by older siblings or younger aunts and uncles.

As the village grew in size, the relationships between members of the community would have changed substantially. For the first century or two, with a population of less than 100 or 150 people, everyone would have known all of their fellow villagers to some extent. But with higher populations, living in a more extensive and densely built-up village, there would have been fewer occasions for face-to-face interaction, and a greater degree of separation. In earlier times interaction between villagers would have been constant and informal, but later more formal systems would have been required to negotiate relationships and decisions, to arrange communal activities and to resolve conflicts.

While there is little or no evidence at Marki for marked differences in social or economic status, the emergence of some households without courtyards in Early Cypriot II may signify an increasing differentiation in land ownership through time. Some households perhaps continued to own land, while families without land engaged in more specialised activities, in which case the latter may have provided a market for the surplus produce of the former and a source of seasonal labour. This situation is likely to have led to an increasing divergence of household activities and to changing and increasingly complex relationships between households.

Herding and Harvesting

Wheat and barley were the primary staples. A wide variety of other plants were also grown or gathered, including legumes (chick peas, lentils and beans) and fruits and nuts such as olives, grapes, figs, almonds and pistachios. These would have been stored in large jars, and perhaps also mudbrick and stone bins.

Sheep and goat were the most common domestic animals at Marki, with the latter increasingly important through time. An analysis of the ages at which animals were killed suggests that they were kept mainly for meat. Nevertheless their other products – milk and wool – would not have been ignored. While sheep of earlier periods in Cyprus resembled the wild moufflon, a new breed appears to have been introduced at the beginning of the Bronze Age. Unlike the older variety, these were woolly, suggesting that wool was now an important product. This is further supported by the introduction of new spinning and weaving equipment at this time.

Cattle, although fewer in number, provided a considerably larger proportion of the meat supply than did sheep and goats. They were, also, important in other ways, especially as work animals. We know from models found at other sites, for example, that they were used to draw ploughs. Another work animal introduced by Bronze Age settlers to Cyprus, and found in the earliest deposits at Marki, was the donkey. Once again, models of the period show its use as a beast of burden. In addition to these domestic animals, wild fallow deer were hunted for meat and their antlers were used for tools and furnishings. Pigs, important in earlier periods, were relatively rare at Marki. Dogs were present in small numbers in all periods at the site, presumably kept as pets or to assist with hunting and herding.

Preparing and Serving Food

While we know something of the ingredients available to the inhabitants of the village at Marki, the recipes and flavours elude us. Wheat and barley seeds were ground into flour, which was collected in clay mealing bins as it fell from the edges of heavy stone querns and rubbers (Fig. 13). Large, shallow pottery basins may also have been used to collect flour, to prepare dough, and to sort and prepare other food. Larger sized bowls with spouts perhaps served to skim or separate liquids, either after soaking legumes or olives or in processing milk.

Figure 13. Upper and lower grindstones (quern and rubber).

In the earliest periods tall deep 'vats' with a central hole in the base may have been used for leaching olives, curing cheese or fermenting other food. Larger jugs were no doubt used for collecting, storing and pouring water and perhaps wine. Smaller vessels may have held condiments or been used as tableware.

Cooking appears to have been done in several different ways. Low-walled circular pans, some of which were supported by three legs, may have been used in ovens for cooking flat bread or with coals for parching wheat, barley or other food. Deeper pans, also sometimes furnished with three legs, perhaps served primarily as braziers, providing a source of light and heat. The presence of ovens suggests that some food was baked or roasted.

Bronze Age cooks also used one- or two-handled cooking pots, specially designed for maximum efficiency and to withstand the stress of constant heating and cooling (Fig. 14). These pots come in different sizes, perhaps used for more individual meals for smaller families or for cooking in larger quantities in larger households or on special occasions. The pots were used over built-in hearths, sometimes supported by distinctive horseshoe-shaped hobs or pot stands (Fig. 15). The relatively small size of the fire-boxes in these hearths suggests that cooking was done over a low heat to prepare soups, stews or porridges, using chick peas, beans or lentils as well as cereals and meat.

Although their form changed slightly over time, small bowls were always the most common vessel at Marki. They were probably used for individual servings of both food and drink. Water was probably the most common beverage, but there may have been others. We have no direct evidence, but several models of daily life from other sites of the period can plausibly be interpreted as showing grape-pressing, for juice or wine.

Figure 14 (left). Cooking pots.

Figure 15 (below). Hob or pot stand.

Arts, Crafts and Industries

Pottery is the most obvious of the items made and used at Marki (Fig. 16). As with all pottery of the prehistoric Bronze Age, vessels were hand-built. A range of shapes was produced to serve different purposes with some specific wares reserved for particular functions – notably the cooking pots.

Figure 16. A selection of storage, cooking and serving vessels, Early Cypriot III and Middle Cypriot I.

The context of manufacture is a key issue. While some poorer quality vessels and those used for special purposes (such as the vats) may have been made at Marki, it is unlikely that most – and especially the finer vessels – were made there in the earliest years. This is suggested both by the small size of the founder population and the fact that the pottery is indistinguishable from that at other sites. At this time, it appears, most pottery was imported. Later, during our Phases C and D (Early Cypriot I–II), the pottery is more distinctive and it is probable that much of it was now made locally, a pattern which continued for the rest of the lifetime of the settlement. The relative numbers of vessels broken and discarded suggests that on average each household needed only half-a-dozen replacement vessels each year: this seems too few to ensure the regularity of production required to learn, develop and maintain skills if every household produced its own pottery. It is likely, therefore, that some families began to specialise in pottery production, exchanging their products for other goods and services provided by their fellow villagers.

Metallurgy was important from the beginning of the settlement. Indeed it was probably the incentive for its establishment. There is little direct evidence of metalworking in the areas excavated, but the presence of three stone casting moulds leaves little doubt that this aspect of the craft was carried out in or beside the village (Fig. 17).

Everyday domestic crafts included spinning and weaving. Spindle whorls of different sizes suggest that flax, wool and perhaps goat hair were spun into thread (Fig. 18). Large heavy clay weights, some weighing more than a kilogram, indicate that cloth was woven on upright warp-weighted looms (Fig. 19).

Passing the Time

On the surface little would have changed over the centuries in the way in which people spent their time. The seasonal cycle dictated agricultural activities, with more intensive periods of work, probably involving all able-bodied people, during the autumn ploughing and sowing season and the spring and summer harvesting. At other times some people (perhaps groups of men) went out from the village to work the copper mines a few kilometres into the Troodos foothills, bringing back processed metal for final casting at home. Some other crafts would also have been seasonal, with pottery production taking place in the summer months; others responded to more immediate needs (such as fashioning and repairing sickles) or were carried out in the intervals of other tasks.

It is not unlikely that the women of the household were responsible for most domestic duties. Much of their time would have been spent working with the heavy rubbers and querns (grindstones) grinding cereals into flour, or preparing other foods. Women were probably also responsible for many other everyday crafts such as spinning wool, hair or flax, weaving the cloth on their warp-weighted looms, and cutting and sewing clothes. These, to judge from the stylised and schematic decoration on plank-shaped figurines, may well have been decorated with simple linear or geometric patterns. Skills would have been acquired at home, by observation, practice and informal training, perhaps passed on from mother to daughter. However, given the relatively short life-span of most people, in many cases it must have been elder sisters, cousins, aunts or step-mothers who were responsible for training the younger children.

Figure 17. Stone moulds for casting copper ingots.

Figure 18. Terracotta spindle whorls.

Figure 19. Clay loomweights.

Much of this work might have taken place in the courtyards of house compounds in the summer, and in the winter months in the crowded interior rooms. Here, hidden behind the enclosing screen walls, were the hearths, normally set within a low plaster fender and flanked by low benches. Bins and emplacements served for storage or as settings for pots or other utensils, while vessels and other equipment may have been placed on shelves on the walls or hung from wooden pegs or deer antlers attached to central roof-posts.

Death, Burial and Ritual

The settlement at Marki was surrounded by a series of cemeteries, for the most part consisting of tombs dug into the sloping ridges of the surrounding chalk hills. In common with other prehistoric Bronze Age people of Cyprus, they hollowed out chambers which were entered through narrow openings which could be blocked by large stone slabs (Fig. 20). The tombs are, however, generally smaller and often less well made than some of those known from larger, richer sites – especially where better quality limestone allowed neater or more elaborate tombs to be carved. One of the cemetery areas at least was in use from the time the village was first established. Philia graves here, and at some other sites, were not chamber tombs but simpler, circular shallow pits (Fig. 21).

The people of Marki shared the common Cypriot Bronze Age custom of placing artefacts alongside the bodies of the dead. Some items, especially complex vessels decorated with relief figures, may have been designed with a funeral in mind, but most vessels can be shown to have been in prior use in the settlement. We do not know why they were placed in tombs. Were they from the house of the dead person, and considered inappropriate for others to use? Were they offerings made by relatives as a sign of respect and relationship? Do they signify the status of the dead person – an indication, perhaps, of their age and gender?

Although burial in the distant cemeteries was the norm, we have a very small number of simple burials within the settlement – generally in the ruins of a long-abandoned building (Fig. 22). It is not clear whether any of these unusual burials were accompanied by grave-goods, but they certainly do not have the quantity or quality of material placed in the cemetery tombs. Where age and sex can be determined, these are seen to be the burials of women, in one case found together with remains of three young children.

Figure 20. A chamber tomb during excavation.

Figure 21. A Philia pit tomb.

Figure 22. Burial of a young woman in the ruins of an abandoned building.

Figure 23. Philia jar burial containing the body of an infant.

In the earliest layers of the site one more unusual burial was found – the remains of a small child, about one year old, placed in an old storage jar which was buried up to the rim in the ground (Fig. 23). Jar burials are extremely rare in Bronze Age Cyprus, but reflect a widespread custom in Anatolia.

Apart from burials we have no clear evidence of other ritual activity at Marki. Modelled scenes – one probably found in a Marki tomb – give an indication of ritual practices, but our excavations found nothing which could justifiably be seen as anything other than normal, everyday behaviour.

Relating to the Wider World

The founders of the village at Marki brought with them both seeds and animals but it is unlikely that they could have been self-sufficient for quite some time. It may have taken several years before there would have been sufficient locally-grown produce to support even so small a community. Several generations would have passed before the village was sufficiently large in size to reduce the need for external marriage partners and to become fully self-sufficient in other ways. Particular crafts, such as pottery manufacture, may have been beyond the skill or ability of the villagers for some time, for it is likely that the bulk of their pottery was brought in from elsewhere. Only simpler, cruder vessels were made in the village. Later, as the population grew, more vessels were locally produced, with only a few exotic items brought in from elsewhere, often as containers for other substances rather than as items in their own right. In return, Marki provided copper, producing both finished products and ingots cast in stone moulds for distribution to centres further from the ore-bearing zone.

As the community increased in size, the nature of internal contacts between the inhabitants of Marki and external connections with neighbours changed. Initially the material culture, economy and symbolism of the village conformed to the cohesive and uniform system seen across most of the island, which we characterise as the Philia culture, the earliest manifestation of the Cypriot Bronze Age. As Bronze Age populations increased, the close links signalled by this material weakened, and more localised, regional variations developed in the Early Cypriot I and II periods. Although now for the most part locally produced, the pottery at Marki bears closest similarity to that of sites in the south or south-east coastal region. Later developments of generically similar wares and the presence of items from central and northern regions show not only the maintenance of close connections of a kind which promoted the spread of new styles and techniques, but also slight shifts in social and economic alliances. Alongside commodities such as copper, these must have involved the regular, if not frequent, movement of people between villages, developing kinship ties which established or enhanced economic links and provided the mechanism for the spread of goods and ideas.

Epilogue

Our excavations at Marki ended in early 2001, after a decade of fieldwork and survey. At this time over 2000 m² of the site had been exposed, leaving by far the greater part of the village still hidden below the modern surface. The excavated area is now fenced and the entire area of the ancient site is protected by legislation from housing and agricultural development, which we hope will preserve it for future generations of archaeologists. After five years of post-excavation research and analysis, a full publication of our results appeared in 2006. The finds are housed in the Cyprus Museum.

In addition to the major funding provided by the Australian Government in the form of three large grants awarded by the Australian Research Council, additional financial assistance for preparing the publication was received from the Mediterranean Archaeology Trust (UK) and the Institute for Aegean Prehistory (USA). Our work has also been generously supported by the Cypriot community of Melbourne and Victoria and colleagues and students at La Trobe University.

Our work in Cyprus continues a long tradition of Australian involvement in Cypriot Bronze Age archaeology, which began with the excavations of Professor James Stewart at Bellapais Vounous in 1937. In 1962 Stewart published the first definitive account of the Early Bronze Age in Cyprus: our research, like that of many others, owes a great deal to his detailed analysis of the history and material culture of this period. We would like to dedicate this small booklet to his widow, Mrs D.E. (Eve) Stewart, who, for over 40 years following her husband's death in 1962, painstakingly prepared his notes on Early and Middle Bronze Age pottery for publication. She managed to complete this task just prior to her own death in December 2005.

Bibliography

T.L. Debney, 1996. Form and function: assemblage variability and use-wear analysis of a flaked stone assemblage from Marki *Alonia*. BA (Honours) Thesis, La Trobe University.

L. Dugay, 1996. Specialized pottery production on Bronze Age Cyprus and pottery use-wear analysis. *Journal of Mediterranean Archaeology* 9.2:167–192.

D. Frankel, 1998. Constructing Marki *Alonia*. Reflections on method and authority in archaeological reporting. *Journal of Mediterranean Archaeology* 11:242–256.

D. Frankel, 2000. Migration and ethnicity in prehistoric Cyprus: technology as *habitus*. *European Journal of Archaeology* 3:167–187.

D. Frankel and J.M. Webb 1994. Hobs and hearths in Bronze Age Cyprus. *Opuscula Atheniensia* XX:51–56.

D. Frankel and J.M. Webb 1995. Archaeological research in the Marki region, 1990. In S.J. Bourke and J.-P. Descoeudres (eds), *Trade, Contact, and the Movement of Peoples in the Eastern Mediterranean: Studies in Honour of J. Basil Hennessy*. Mediterranean Archaeology Supplementary Vol. 3, Sydney, pp. 115–128.

D. Frankel and J.M. Webb, 1996. *Marki Alonia. An Early and Middle Bronze Age Town in Cyprus. Excavations 1990–1994*. Studies in Mediterranean Archaeology CXXIII:1. Jonsered: Paul Åströms Förlag.

D. Frankel and J.M. Webb, 2001. Population, households and ceramic consumption in a prehistoric Cypriot village. *Journal of Field Archaeology* 28:115-129.

D. Frankel and J.M. Webb, 2006. Neighbours. Negotiating space in a prehistoric village. *Antiquity* 80:287–302.

D. Frankel and J.M. Webb, 2006. *Marki Alonia. An Early and Middle Bronze Age Settlement in Cyprus. Excavations 1995–2000*. Studies in Mediterranean Archaeology CXXIII:2. Sävedalen: Paul Åströms Förlag.

A.C. Sneddon, 2002. *The Cemeteries at Marki: Using a Looted Landscape to Investigate Prehistoric Bronze Age Cyprus*. BAR International Series, No. 1028. Oxford: Archaeopress

J.M. Webb, 1994. Techniques of pottery manufacture at Marki Alonia. *Archaeologia Cypria* III:12–21.

J.M. Webb 1995. Abandonment processes and curate/discard strategies at Marki-*Alonia*, Cyprus. *The Artefact* 18:64–70.

J.M. Webb, 1998. Lithic technology and discard at Marki, Cyprus: consumer behaviour and site formation in the prehistoric Bronze Age. *Antiquity* 72:796–805.

J.M. Webb, 1998. Engendering the built environment: household and community in prehistoric Bronze Age Cyprus. In D. Bolger and N. Serwint (eds) *Engendering Aphrodite: Women and Society in Ancient Cyprus*, pp. 87–101. American Schools of Oriental Research Archaeological Reports 7, Cyprus American Archaeological Institute Monographs 3. Boston.

J.M. Webb, 2002. *Exploring Bronze Age Cyprus. Australian Perspectives.* University of New England, Armidale.

J.M. Webb, 2006. Material culture and the value of context: a case study from Cyprus. In D. Papaconstantinou (ed), *Deconstructing Context: A Critical Approach to Archaeological Practice*, pp. 98–119. Oxford: Oxbow Books.

J.M. Webb, Keeping house: our developing understanding of the Early and Middle Cypriot household (1926–2006). *Medelhavsmuseet. Focus on the Mediterranean*, Stockholm.

J.M. Webb and D. Frankel, 1999. Characterizing the Philia facies. Material culture, chronology and the origin of the Bronze Age in Cyprus. *American Journal of Archaeology* 103:3–43.

J.M. Webb and D. Frankel, 2001. Clay cattle from Marki. Iconography and ideology in Early and Middle Bronze Age Cyprus. *Archaeologia Cypria* 4:71–82.

J.M. Webb and D. Frankel, 2004. Intensive site survey. Implications for estimating settlement size, population and duration in Prehistoric Bronze Age Cyprus. In M. Iacovou (ed), *Archaeological Field Survey in Cyprus. Past History, Future Potentials*, pp. 125–137. London: British School at Athens Studies 11.

J.M. Webb and D. Frankel, 2004. Prehistoric cooking pots from Cyprus. *Ceramics Technical* 19:91–96.

J.M. Webb and D. Frankel, 2006. Identifying population movements by everyday practice. The case of third millennium Cyprus. In S. Antoniadou and A. Pace (eds), *Mediterranean Crossroads*, Athens: Pierides Foundation.

J.M. Webb, D. Frankel, S. Stos and N. Gale, 2006. Early Bronze Age metal trade in the eastern Mediterranean. New compositional and lead isotope evidence from Cyprus. *Oxford Journal of Archaeology* 25:261–288.

DAVID FRANKEL studied archaeology at the University of Sydney and Gothenburg University, where he specialised in Cypriot prehistory. After some years in the Department of Western Asiatic Antiquities, The British Museum, he returned to Australia in 1978 to take up a lectureship at La Trobe University, where he is now Reader in Archaeology. In 1993 he was elected a Fellow of the Australian Academy of the Humanities, and from 1996 to 1998 served on the Humanities Panel of the Australian Research Council. His research interests include Australian Aboriginal archaeology, with particular reference to south-eastern Australia, and the archaeology of Bronze Age Cyprus. He has excavated a range of sites in Papua New Guinea, Australia and Cyprus, the most important of which is Marki.

JENNIFER M. WEBB is a graduate of the University of Melbourne, where she completed a PhD on ritual practice in Late Bronze Age Cyprus in 1988, later published as *Ritual Architecture, Iconography and Practice in the Late Cypriot Bronze Age*. Studies in Mediterranean Archaeology and Literature Pocketbook 75. Paul Åströms Förlag, Göteborg 1999. She has published extensively on Cypriot archaeology, including several volumes on Cypriot antiquities in Australian collections, and co-directed the excavations at Marki with David Frankel. For the last 15 years she has been associated with La Trobe University in Melbourne, including five years as an Australian Research Council Research Fellow. She is currently a Charles Joseph La Trobe Fellow. She was elected a Fellow of the Australian Academy of the Humanities in 2001. In addition to her archaeological interests, she is the Senior Moderator of the Cranlana Programme, an executive leadership seminar based in Melbourne.